Fact Finders

ACTION SCIENCE

THE SCIENCE OF LIGHTING A CITY
ELECTRICITY IN ACTION

by Jim Whiting

Consultant:
Paul Ohmann, PhD
Associate Professor of Physics
University of St. Thomas, St. Paul, Minnesota

CAPSTONE PRESS
a capstone imprint

Fact Finders is published by Capstone Press,
1710 Roe Crest Drive, North Mankato, Minnesota 56003.
www.capstonepress.com

Library of Congress Cataloging-in-Publication Data
Whiting, Jim, 1943–
    The science of lighting a city: electricity in action / by Jim Whiting.
    p. cm. — (Fact finders. Action science.)
    Summary:"Describes the science behind electricity, including generation and transmission"— Provided
by publisher.
    Includes bibliographical references and index.
    ISBN 978-1-4296-3954-5 (library binding)
    ISBN 978-1-4296-4856-1 (paperback)
    1. Water-power — Juvenile literature. 2. Hydroelectric power plants — Juvenile literature.
3. Electricity — Juvenile literature. I. Title. II. Series.
TC147.W45 2010
621.31 — dc22   2009033240

Editorial Credits
Lori Shores, editor; Lori Bye, designer; Jo Miller, media researcher; Eric Manske, production specialist

Photo Credits:
Capstone Press/Juliette Peters, 7
Capstone Studio/Karon Dubke, 15, 18, 19, 20
Getty Images Inc./FoodPix/Burke/Triolo Productions, 5; SuperStock, 9
iStockphoto/Ryan Kelly, 11
Library of Congress, 28 (top)
Photo Researchers, Inc/David R. Frazier, 27
Shutterstock/Aaron Kohr, 6; Andrea Danti, 8; Bob Reynolds, 24; CAN BALCIOGLU, 22; DDCoral, 13; dragon_
    fang, 14; emin kuliyev, cover; FERNANDO BLANCO CALZADA, 29 (bottom); frank ungrad, 16–17;
    Laurence Gough, 25 (bottom); Marta P., 25 (top); PavleMarjanovic, 23; qhl1208, 10; Ratko M, 2–3 (design
    element); Sebastian Kaulitzki, 29 (top); Tiffany Chan, 26
Visuals Unlimited/Patrice Ceisel, 28 (bottom)

Essential content terms are **bold** and are defined at the bottom of the page where they first appear.

Printed in the United States of America in Stevens Point, Wisconsin.
082013
007683R

TABLE OF CONTENTS

EVERYDAY ELECTRICITY

You wake to the buzzing of an alarm clock. You flip on the lights and take a nice warm shower. In the kitchen, you reach into the refrigerator for milk. You pop slices of bread into the toaster.

But what if the electricity goes out? Your alarm clock wouldn't go off. Your room would be dark. You'd have no hot shower or toast. You'd soon realize how much you depend on electricity.

Even if you don't see it, electricity is everywhere. But to use electricity to light your city, you need science. Science brings electricity from the power plant to the city and keeps it running smoothly in your home. Every time you turn on a light, you witness the science of electricity in action.

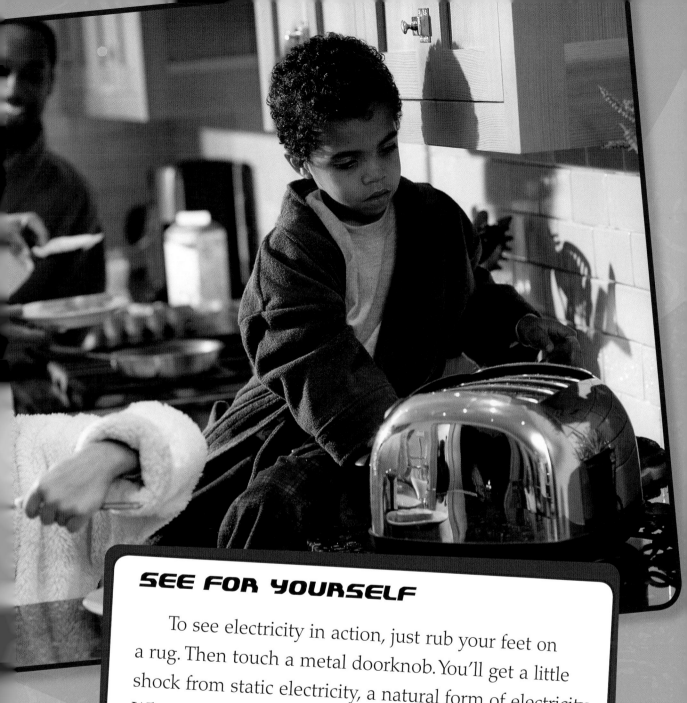

SEE FOR YOURSELF

To see electricity in action, just rub your feet on a rug. Then touch a metal doorknob. You'll get a little shock from static electricity, a natural form of electricity. When you rub your feet on the rug, you build up an electric charge. The electricity transfers to the metal when you touch the doorknob.

CHAPTER 1

MAKING ELECTRICITY

Before you flip the light switch, science has brought your electricity a long way. Follow that electricity back to the source, and you'll end up at a power plant. You might be surprised to find that making electricity starts with boiling water.

Large power plants make electricity for cities and surrounding areas.

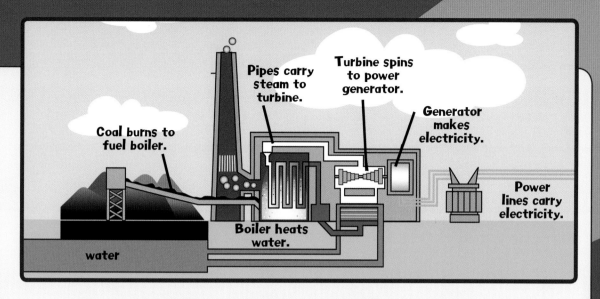

Coal burns to fuel boiler.

Pipes carry steam to turbine.

Turbine spins to power generator.

Generator makes electricity.

Power lines carry electricity.

Boiler heats water.

water

Many power plants burn coal to heat water. Other plants use nuclear energy, natural gas, or oil. No matter what fuel the plants use, the key is to boil water so it turns into steam. Thick pipes carry the steam to **turbines** in another part of the power plant. The steam pushes past the blades of the turbines. The blades spin rapidly, like a fan.

The turbines are connected to **generators**. These large machines produce electricity. Inside the generator, there is a large magnet surrounded by a coil of wire. As the turbine blades spin, the magnet spins, and the science of electricity begins.

—————•———————

turbine — a machine in which a flowing liquid or gas turns a set of blades

generator — a machine that produces electricity

Everything around you is made of tiny bits of matter called atoms. Atoms are made up of a central core, or nucleus. **Electrons** move around the nucleus. Electrons have an electric charge. When the generator's magnet spins, it pulls electrons free from the atoms of the wire coil around it. The loose electrons bump into other atoms, sending more electrons flying. In just a fraction of a second, billions of electrons move along the wire, creating an electric **current**.

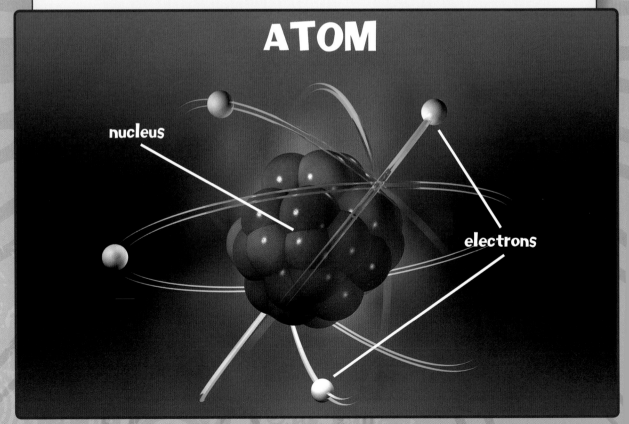

ATOM

nucleus

electrons

Every spin of the generator produces more electricity. The electricity flows along the wire coil in a constant stream. At the end of the coil, the wire straightens out, carrying the electricity out of the generator. This electric current will eventually light up your city, but it still has a long journey.

—————◆—————

electron — a tiny part of an atom that carries an electric charge

current — a flow of electricity made by electrons passing through a wire

The First Power Plant

Thomas Edison invented electric lightbulbs in 1879. But people needed a steady source of electricity to use the new lights. So in 1882, Edison built the world's first power plant in New York City. He had wires strung directly from the plant to houses. On the first day, Edison's power plant supplied power to 85 homes with a total of 400 lights.

Thomas Edison

CHAPTER 2

FROM POWER PLANT TO YOU

When the electricity leaves the generator, it is very powerful at around 10,000 **volts**. But before it heads to your city, the electricity needs a boost. Many power plants are 100 miles (161 kilometers) or more from the cities they serve. To travel all that way, the voltage must be even stronger.

power lines —

These large towers support power lines carrying electricity to your city.

transformer

Transformers that raise voltage
are called step-up transformers.

A **transformer** next to the power plant
gives electricity the boost it needs to travel.
Transformers raise and lower the voltage
of electricity that is sent through them. The
transformer at the power plant raises the voltage.
When it leaves the transformer, the electricity
is at 350,000 volts. The voltage is now strong
enough to push the current on its way.

The electricity begins its journey through
thick cables. Sometimes the heavy cables are
strung high above the ground. But power lines
can also be underground.

voltage — the strength with which an electric current is pushed;
voltage is measured in volts.

transformer — a machine that raises or lowers voltage

High voltage is great when a current has a long way to go. But this voltage is too strong to use at home. An electric current at 350,000 volts would fry all the wires in your home and start a fire. After the long trip, the current passes through a transformer at one of the **substations** around your city. The substation transformer lowers the voltage to about 7,000 volts. The voltage is still too high for your house, but it is just right for traveling across the city.

The electricity is now ready to be sent all over your city. Wires mounted overhead on wooden poles lead from substations to major roads. More wires branch out to every street in the city. The wires carry the electricity to stores, movie theaters, homes, and any place that needs power.

transformer

substation — a small building or fenced-in area containing equipment to control the flow of electricity to a nearby area

Substation

transformer

Workers turn off the power to a transformer before they make repairs. Their hard work keeps the electricity flowing smoothly.

CHAPTER 3

AROUND AND AROUND

You can see a transformer without leaving your yard. Just look for the metal drum near the top of the nearest power pole.

The long journey from the power plant to your home is nearly over. But as the current races from the substation, it is still too strong to use at home. Almost everything in your home, from your desk lamp to the TV, operates with around 110 volts of electricity. Major appliances such as washers and dryers need 220 volts. One last trip through a transformer lowers the voltage again.

The current has a final stop before it enters your home. The wires coming from the transformer go through a meter. The meter records how much electricity passes into your house. The meter also measures how much electricity you use at home. Then the electric company charges you for the electricity used each month.

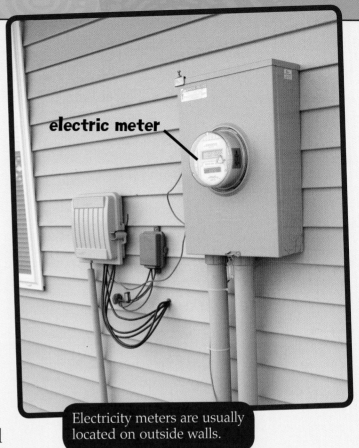

electric meter

Electricity meters are usually located on outside walls.

SEE FOR YOURSELF

Following the path of your electrical power is a fun activity. First try to guess how far away the substation is. Then find the wires leading from your house to the pole next to the street. Have your parents drive along the route the wires take. At the end, you'll find the substation serving your neighborhood.

Household Wiring

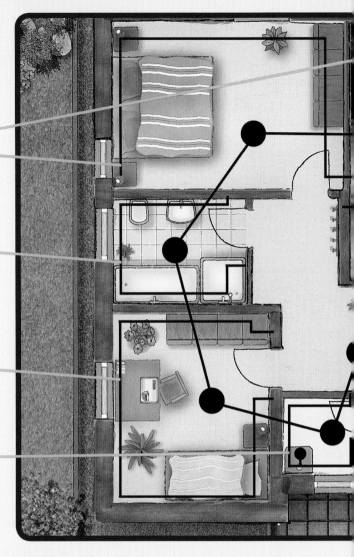

Outlets in the bedroom and living room share a circuit.

Bathroom circuit uses special outlets that shut down if they get wet.

Bedrooms can also be on their own circuits.

A laundry room has two circuits. The electric dryer is on its own circuit.

Finally the current flows into your home. But it doesn't just go anywhere it wants. The electricity is first divided up into 110-volt and 220-volt wires. These wires spread through your home, carrying electricity to the lights and appliances you use every day.

Outdoor circuit uses special outlets that shut down if they get wet.

Overhead lights are all on one circuit.

Kitchen circuit can cover all outlets other than the one for the stove.

Electric stove is on its own circuit.

The wires in your house are divided into circuits, or paths, for electricity to flow through. A circuit makes a loop to one area of the house and back to the main power box. It carries only enough electricity to supply the needs of one room or appliance. Circuits limit the amount of electricity that flows through wires at one time.

For the electric current to flow, a circuit has to be complete. You break and connect circuits all the time. For example, one circuit powers your bedroom. When the light switch is in the off position, the circuit is broken. The current stops flowing. When you flip the switch on, the circuit is connected. The current flows, and the light comes on.

All the circuits in your house start and end at the main power box.

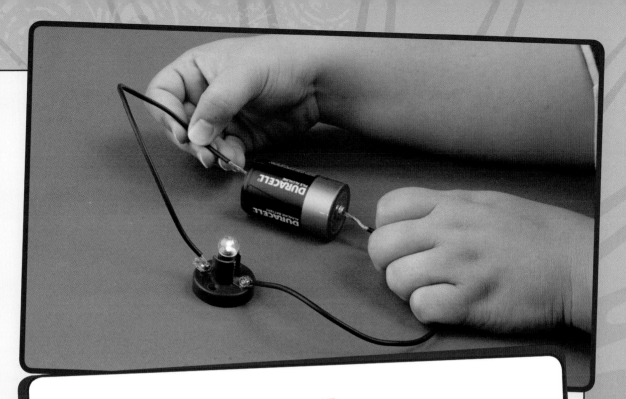

SEE FOR YOURSELF

To make a simple circuit, you'll need two 1-foot (0.3 meter) pieces of electrical wire. You'll also need a size D (1.5-volt) battery, a 1.5-volt lightbulb, and a bulb holder. Have an adult help you remove the rubber from both ends of the electrical wires. Fasten one end of each wire to the bulb holder. Carefully hold the wires with your fingers only touching the rubber coating. Touch the other end of one wire to one end of the battery. Now touch the other end of the second wire to the other end of the battery to complete the loop. The bulb lights up. When you remove one wire, the circuit is broken, and the bulb turns off.

One afternoon, you're working on your computer in your bedroom. All the lights are on. You're listening to music and printing your homework. Then your mom decides to vacuum your carpet. As soon as she turns the vacuum on, everything goes dark. You're using more electricity in your room than the circuit can handle.

Electrical circuits can only handle a certain amount of electricity. Sometimes there is too much demand for electricity on one circuit. Then a circuit breaker stops the flow of electricity so the wires don't overheat. Once the problem has been corrected, the circuit breaker can be reset. Electricity then flows through the wires again.

CHAPTER 4

KEEPING UP WITH DEMAND

Every year, the need for electricity increases. Earth's population continues to grow. New homes and businesses pop up all over. Everything seems to need electricity, and that means more power plants. But power plants that use fossil fuels to heat water create air pollution. And power plants that use nuclear energy create nuclear waste, which is dangerous. To keep the environment healthy, people need clean sources of **renewable energy**.

Water flows through turbines to power generators in the powerhouse.

Water pools behind dam.

Transformers raise voltage and send current to power lines.

One source of clean, renewable energy is hydroelectric power. This power comes from damming rivers. Water flows through the dam and drives turbines to produce electricity. There's no air pollution or dangerous materials. But hydroelectric power can only be developed in areas with major rivers.

renewable energy — power from sources that can never be used up, such as wind and the sun

Scientists are developing more ways to make electricity. Wind power is an energy source that is used more and more every year. Wind turns the blades of tall wind turbines. The turning blades power generators, just like in power plants. Single homes and businesses can use small turbines for their power.

wind turbines

Areas with plenty of sunshine can use the sun to make electricity. Solar power is used to heat water for steam that powers turbines and generators. Some solar power panels can make electricity directly from sunlight.

solar panels

Geothermal energy uses heat from deep inside the earth. In some areas, this heat causes steam to rise from the ground. The steam is piped directly to turbines, where it turns the blades to power generators.

geothermal power plant

Using less electricity also helps the environment by saving natural resources. If everyone used less, fewer power plants would be needed, and less coal and oil would be used. You can do your part to save energy by wearing sweaters instead of turning up the heat. Taking shorter showers saves on electricity used to heat your water. Even turning off the TV when no one is watching cuts down on electrical use. By using only what they need, people share the benefits of electricity and save money. And saving electricity shows respect for the science that delivers electricity to cities every day.

The Electric Grid

Millions of homes, businesses, factories, parks, stadiums, and other places need electricity. The electric grid helps to make sure they all get the power they need. The grid connects all the power plants and power lines within a certain area. Sometimes an area served by one power plant needs more electricity than usual. If the plant in that area can't keep up, electricity is borrowed from other power plants through the grid.

About 200,000 miles (321,869 kilometers) of power lines make up the electric grid in the United States.

ELECTRIC FACTS

• Telephone and cable TV companies often use the same poles that carry your electricity.

Benjamin Franklin's kite experiment

• In 1752, Benjamin Franklin flew a kite in a thunderstorm. It was a very dangerous experiment, but it proved that lightning is a form of electricity.

• In some areas, power lines are buried. These underground wires are safer, but they're also more expensive to put in place.

• The word electricity comes from an ancient Greek word that means amber. Amber is hardened tree sap. The Greeks rubbed pieces of amber on fur or wool to make static electricity.

• Electric eels make electricity in their bodies. They use the electricity to kill prey.

electric eel

OTHER SCIENCES IN ACTION

The Human Body — Your body uses electricity, but you don't need to be plugged in. Nerve cells carry electrical signals to and from your brain. The signals allow you to move and feel pain.

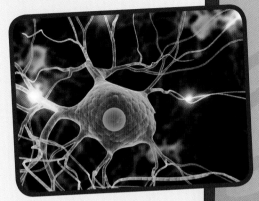

Nuclear Energy — To create nuclear energy, the nucleus of an atom is split. This action releases particles called neutrons. The neutrons strike other atoms and split their centers. This chain reaction produces heat to boil water and make steam.

Battery Power — Most batteries are made up of a carbon rod inside a zinc case. Chemicals surround

the carbon rod. Electrons flow from the carbon rod through the chemicals to the zinc walls. When the battery is attached to a circuit, the electric current flows out of the battery.

Glossary

atom (AT-uhm) — an element in its smallest form

current (KUHR-uhnt) — a flow of electricity made by electrons passing through a wire

electron (i-LEK-tron) — a tiny part of an atom that carries an electric charge

generator (JEN-uh-ray-tuhr) — a machine that produces electricity by turning a magnet inside a coil of wire

renewable energy (ri-NOO-uh-buhl EN-er-jee) — power from sources that will not be used up, such as wind, water, and the sun

substation (SUHB-stay-shuhn) — a small building or fenced-in area containing equipment to control the flow of electricity to a nearby area

transformer (trans-FOR-muhr) — a machine that raises or lowers the voltage of an electric current

turbine (TUHR-buhn) — a device in which a flowing liquid or gas turns a set of blades; turbines range from simple windmills and waterwheels to giant electric generators.

voltage (VOL-tij) — the strength with which an electric current is pushed; voltage is measured in volts.

Read More

Moore, Rob. *Why Does Electricity Flow?* Solving Science Mysteries. New York: PowerKids Press, 2010.

O'Donnell, Liam. *The Shocking World of Electricity With Max Axiom, Super Scientist.* Graphic Science. Mankato, Minn.: Capstone Press, 2007.

Ollhoff, Jim. *Wind and Water.* Future Energy. Edina, Minn.: Abdo, 2010.

Spilsbury, Richard and Louise Spilsbury. *What Is Electricity and Magnetism?: Exploring Science with Hands-On Activities.* In Touch with Basic Science. Berkeley Heights, N.J.: Enslow, 2008.

Internet Sites

FactHound offers a safe, fun way to find Internet sites related to this book. All of the sites on FactHound have been researched by our staff.

Here's all you do:

Visit *www.facthound.com*

FactHound will fetch the best sites for you!

Index